—THE PLAN FOR NONBELIEVERS —
FROM **DARK**
TO **LIGHT**

AND THE RESISTANCE AGAINST IT

Never Revealed History of a
Friend of Medjugorje and the
Second of the Month Messages.

Compiled by Caritas of Birmingham

With an Epilogue by A Friend of Medjugorje

─THE PLAN FOR NONBELIEVERS ─

FROM DARK

TO LIGHT

AND THE RESISTANCE AGAINST IT

Never Revealed History of a
Friend of Medjugorje and the
Second of the Month Messages.

Compiled by Caritas of Birmingham

With an Epilogue by A Friend of Medjugorje

SPECIAL STATEMENT

Caritas of Birmingham is not acting on behalf of the Catholic Church or placing its mission under the Church. Its mission is to reach all people of the earth. Its actions are outside of the Church done privately. It is further stated:

So as not to take for granted the credibility of the Medjugorje Apparitions, it is stated that the Medjugorje apparitions are not formally approved by the Catholic Church.

Medjugorje Status
May 25, 2020 A.D.

No attempt is intended to pre-empt the Church on the validity of the Medjugorje Apparitions. They are private revelation waiting the Church's final judgment[1]. In the interim, these private revelations **are** allowed by, and for, the faithful to have devotion to and to be spread legally by the Church. Devotion and the propagation of private revelations can be forbidden only **if** the private revelation is condemned because of anything it contains which contravenes faith and morals according to AAS 58 (1966) 1186 Congregation for the Doctrine of the Faith. Medjugorje has not been condemned nor found to have anything against faith or morals, therefore it is in the grace of the Church to be followed by the faithful. By the rite of Baptism one is commissioned and given the authority to evangelize. *"By Baptism they share in the priesthood of Christ, in His prophetic and royal mission."*[2] One does not need approval to promote or to have devotions to private revelations or to spread them when in conformity to AAS 58 (1966) 1186, as the call to evangelize is given when baptized. These apparitions have not been approved formally by the Church. Caritas of Birmingham, the Community of Caritas and all associated with it, realize and accept that the final authority regarding the Queen of Peace, Medjugorje and happenings related to the apparitions, rests with the Holy See in Rome. We at Caritas, willingly submit to that judgment. While having an amiable relationship with the Diocese of Birmingham and a friendly relationship with its bishop, Caritas of Birmingham as a lay mission is not officially connected to the Diocese of Birmingham, Alabama, just as is the Knights of Columbus.[3] The Diocese of Birmingham's official position on Caritas is neutral and holds us as Catholics in good standing.

1. The Church does not have to approve the apparitions. The Church can do as She did with the apparitions of Rue du Bac in Paris and the Miraculous Medal. The Church never approved these apparitions. She gave way to the people's widespread acceptance of the Miraculous Medal and thereby the Apparitions to St. Catherine. *Sensus Fidelium* (Latin, meaning "The Sense of the Faithful"), regarding Medjugorje, is that the "sense" of the people says that "Mary is here (Medjugorje)."
2. Catechism of the Catholic Church Second Edition.
3. The Knights of Columbus also are not officially under the Church, yet they are very Catholic. The Knights of Columbus was founded as a lay organization in 1882, with the basic Catholic beliefs. Each local council appeals to the local Ordinary to be the Chaplain. The Knights of Columbus is still a lay organization, and operates with its own autonomy.

To Order More Copies of
The Plan for Nonbelievers from Dark to Light
and the Resistance Against It BF127
CALL: Caritas of Birmingham
205-672-2000 ext. 315 twenty-four hours
or order on **mej.com** click on *"Shop Online"*
and click on *"Books by a Friend of Medjugorje"*

About the Witness

Many who will read these books have been following the writings of a Friend of Medjugorje for years. His original and unique insights into the important events of our day have won credence in hundreds of thousands of hearts around the world, with those affecting others, thereby, touching into the millions. His moral courage in the face of so many leaders caving in to the pressures of a politically correct world is not only refreshing, but, according to tens of thousands of written testimonies over 32 years, has helped to strengthen deeply those who desire to live the fullness of their Christian faith. His insights have repeatedly proven prophetic, having their source in the apparitions of the Virgin Mary in Medjugorje. Deeply and personally influenced by the events surrounding Medjugorje, he gave himself to the prayerful application of the words of the Virgin Mary into his life. He has spoken all over the world on Our Lady's messages and how to put them into everyday life. He came to understand that Our Lady was sent by God to speak to mankind in this time because the dangers man is facing are on a scale unlike any the world has ever known since Noah and the flood. He is not an author. He is a witness of what Our Lady has shown him to testify to—first, by his life—secondly, through the written word. He is not one looking in from the outside regarding Medjugorje, but one who is close to the events—many times, right in the middle of the events about which he has written.

Originally writing to only a few individuals in 1987, readership has grown well into the millions in the United States and in over 130 foreign countries, who follow the spiritual insights and direction given through these writings.

When asked why he signs only as "a Friend of Medjugorje," he stated:

> *"I have never had an ambition or desire to write. I do so only because God has shown me, through prayer, that He desires this of me. So from the beginning, when I was writing to only a few people, I prayed to God and promised I would not sign anything; that the writings would have to carry themselves and not*

be built on a personality. I prayed that if it was
God's desire for these writings to be inspired and
known, then He could do it by His Will and grace
and that my will be abandoned to it.

"The Father has made these writings known and
continues to spread them to the ends of the earth.
These were Our Lord's last words before ascend-
ing: ***'Be a witness to the ends of the earth.'*** *These*
writings give testimony to that desire of Our Lord,
to be a witness with one's life. It is not important
to be known. It is important to do God's Will."

For those who require "ownership" of these writings by
the 'witness' in seeing his name printed on this work in
order to give it more credibility, we, Caritas of Birmingham and the Community of Caritas, state that we cannot
reconcile the fact that these writings are producing
hundreds of thousands of conversions, and will easily be
into the millions, through God's grace. His writings are
requested worldwide from every corner of the earth.
His witness and testimony, therefore, will not take credit
for a work that, by proof of the impact these writings
have to lead hearts to conversion, has been Spirit–in-

spired, with numbers increasing yearly, sweeping as a wave across the ocean. Indeed, in this case, crossing every ocean of the earth. Our Lady gave this Witness a direct message, through the Medjugorje visionary, Marija, and part of what Our Lady said to him was to **"...witness not with words but through humility..."** (Oct. 6, 1986) It is for this reason that he wishes to remain simply, "A Friend of Medjugorje."

In order to silence the voice of this witness, darkness has continually spewed out slanders to prevent souls from reading his convicting and life-changing writings. For if these writings were not so, darkness would ignore them or even lead people to them. But Jesus promised persecution to all those who follow Him, and the same will be to those who follow His Mother. *"If they persecuted me, they will also persecute you."* John 15:20

As a witness in real-time of Our Lady's time on earth, his witness and writings will continue to speak—voicing Our Lady's Way to hundreds of millions not yet born—in the centuries to come.

— Caritas of Birmingham

Medjugorje

The Story in Brief

A VILLAGE SEES THE LIGHT is the title of a story which "Reader's Digest" published in February 1986. It was the first major news on a mass public scale that told of the Virgin Mary visiting the tiny village of Medjugorje, Bosnia-Hercegovina. At that time this village was populated by 400 families.

It was June 24, 1981, the Feast of John the Baptist, the proclaimer of the coming Messiah. In the evening, around 5:00 p.m., the Virgin Mary appeared to two young people, Mirjana Dragičević* and Ivanka Ivanković*. Around 6:40 p.m. the same day, Mirjana and Ivanka, along with four more young people, Milka Pavlović*, the little sister of Marija, Ivan Ivanković, Vicka Ivanković*, and Ivan Dragičević saw the Virgin Mary. The next day, June 25, 1981, along with Mirjana, Ivanka, Vicka and Ivan Dragičević, Marija Pavlović* and Jakov Čolo also saw the Virgin Mary, bringing the total to six visionaries. Milka Pavlović* and Ivan Ivanković only saw Our Lady once, on that first day. These six have become known as and remain "the visionaries."

These visionaries are not related to one another. Three of the six visionaries no longer see Our Lady on a

* Names at the time of the apparitions, they are now married with last names changed.

vii

daily basis. As of May 2020, the Virgin is still appearing everyday to the remaining three visionaries; that's well over 16,735 apparitions. This count is each day for all the visionaries together in the apparitions. The visionaries have been separated for more years than together, which means the number is minimum 30 years × 3 visionaries who still see Our Lady daily being separated during apparition time.

The supernatural event has survived all efforts of the Communists to put a stop to it, many scientific studies, and even the condemnation by the local bishop; yet, the apparitions have survived, giving strong evidence that this is from God because nothing and no one has been able to stop it. For over 39 years, the apparitions have proved themselves over and over and now credibility is so favorable around the world that the burden of proof that this is authentic has shifted from those who believe to the burden of proof that it is not happening by those opposed to it. Those against the apparitions are being crushed by the fruits of Medjugorje — millions and millions of conversions which are so powerful that they are changing and will continue to change the whole face of the earth.

See **mej.com** for more information.
or **Medjugorje.com**

ACKNOWLEDGEMENT

God alone deserves the credit for the publication of this book. It is from Him that the messages are allowed to be given through Our Lady to all of mankind. He alone deserves the praise and honor.

Table of Contents

Foreword

Our Lady said in Medjugorje on July 24, 1989:

"...I need you, dear children, to cooperate with me, because there are today many plans that I cannot fulfill without you..."

Over the course of 34+* years, a Friend of Medjugorje, also known as the founder of Caritas of Birmingham and the Community of Caritas, has seen that Our Lady has many plans going on in the world. When Our Lady came to Medjugorje, She did not come blindly, but She came with a plan. Her plan would require many people to walk down different paths and fulfill different functions for the fulfillment of Her plans. Before Our Lady came to the home of a Friend of Medjugorje and his wife in Alabama, in 1988, She had laid a foundation ahead of time, to bring about the effect She desired, for the fulfillment of Her overall strategy against evil. This book will walk you through the evolution of just one of the plans, never before told until now.

* As of May 2020.

"The world is sleeping...we need to stop our sleep and try to follow Our Lady's messages right now!!! There are so many new things to learn in this book!! Thanks a lot to a Friend of Medjugorje for his time and work!!!"

Sudbury, Ontario, Canada

Testimony on <u>From Dark to Light</u>

2

CHAPTER ONE

Turn Back the Clock...

A Friend of Medjugorje often tells a story from the early years of the apparitions, when Mirjana asked Our Lady for a sign. Our Lady responded to Mirjana by smiling. After the apparition, Mirjana noticed that her watch had turned backwards. A Friend of Medjugorje has explained this story many times. We are not focusing on that story here, but rather, we want to take this opportunity to "turn back the clock" for you...

It was January 2, 1997. Medjugorje visionary Mirjana had been receiving inner locutions with Our Lady on the Second of the Month, since August 2, 1987, during which she was being guided by

Our Lady towards her future mission for nonbelievers. Inner locutions mean that Mirjana could see
and hear Our Lady in an interior way, not like the
normal apparitions that the other visionaries were
experiencing, where Our Lady is physically present before them. Mirjana's experiences were also
always in private. We know that on occasion, Our
Lady would appear to Mirjana in a normal apparition, though Our Lady would not forewarn Mirjana
on these special occasions. But, on this day, it was
different. On January 2, 1997, Mirjana was told by
Our Lady in an inner locution, that next month on
February 2, 1997, She would appear to Mirjana at
11:00 AM, Medjugorje time in an apparition. What
did this mean that we suddenly knew that Our Lady
would be coming ahead of time, at an exact time?

To answer this question, we need to first
turn back the clock a few more months. A Friend
of Medjugorje had an in-depth conversation with
Mirjana in March 1996 in which he learned many

new things concerning Mirjana's apparitions.*
The transcript of that conversation/interview was
released in the Caritas Field Angel Newsletter of
July/September 1996 under the title, *Mirjana, A
Mystery is Revealed*. Before it went to press, he
wanted Mirjana to read it to make sure everything
he wrote was correct. He sent two senior community members to Mirjana's house in Medjugorje
with the writing. They spoke with Mirjana on her
front porch, reminding her of her conversation
with a Friend of Medjugorje and presented her
with a copy of his writing, explaining that a Friend
of Medjugorje wanted her to read it to make sure
everything in it was correct. He wanted Mirjana to
point out anything he may have said in error, so he
could make the changes before publishing the writing. Mirjana agreed and, after a few days, when the
community members returned, Mirjana told them

* From the mid-1980s and onward, a Friend of Medjugorje frequently attended
Mirjana's talks to pilgrims, as well as when she spoke to his own groups who came
with Caritas/BVM Pilgrimages. He would document what Mirjana said. On occasion, he also had the opportunity to interview Mirjana personally.

that everything in it was correct. She found no errors in the writing at all.

This writing laid open for the first time, on a worldwide scale, Our Lady's pleading call for prayers for nonbelievers. Mirjana had shared with a Friend of Medjugorje, during his March 1996 conversation with her, details about a secret prayer that Our Lady had taught her. Mirjana had been praying this prayer with Our Lady on the second of each month for the conversion of nonbelievers. According to Mirjana, this prayer, though not one of the secrets, is at the same time connected to the secrets. It is important to note that a Friend of Medjugorje learned later that others knew about this secret prayer of Mirjana for nonbelievers before he learned of it, but it never became "known" among Medjugorje followers. Doing research over the years, a Friend of Medjugorje discovered knowledge of this prayer buried deep in a few books no longer in print. This was big news, yet no one was spreading it. That changed through the July/September 1996 Caritas Newsletter. A Friend of Medjugorje informed tens of thousands of people around the world, for the first time, about the prayers and the importance of praying for nonbelievers. As people became informed, they began responding by praying for Our Lady's intentions for nonbelievers.

In *Mirjana, A Mystery is Revealed*, a Friend of Medjugorje wrote a prayer that he titled, *Prayer for Nonbelievers*, which rose from the concern he felt for nonbelievers after learning from Mirjana *how concerned Our Lady is* for these souls, whom She said are nonbelievers because they do not know and/or have never experienced, the love of God. A Friend of Medjugorje became filled with the desire to see the release of Our Lady's prayer that She had revealed to Mirjana. The *Prayer for Nonbelievers* was embraced around the world. Today, it is still being given out by the thousands in Medjugorje

through the Caritas Mission House, through re-
quests made to Caritas in Alabama, and through
the Caritas website, Medjugorje.com. Many people
have been praying this prayer for years every Second of the Month, especially for family members.
As you read the *Prayer for Nonbelievers*, realize,
again, that at the time a Friend of Medjugorje wrote
it, Our Lady had not yet given Mirjana any hint
that the Second of the Month inner locutions would
soon become apparitions and that Our Lady would
begin to open up Mirjana's apparitions to everyone
to attend who wanted to be present. With that in
mind, read carefully what he was asking for in this
Prayer for Nonbelievers.

Prayer for Nonbelievers

*Come Mary, come tomorrow again and
again. We will pray with you. Bring back
our loved ones who have left the Church,
those who have left God. We will join you on*

the second of each month. We will pray for greater graces to be attached to your intention. We will pray that the dam of love, of God's mercy, will break forth, that your new prayer* be released soon. We will pray that it will flow out as a river to all the nations, that as the rivers fill the oceans, your love of God will fill the earth. We wait. We anticipate that great day, and we call you as you have called us, to add our prayers, fasting and sacrifices to Mirjana's, in order that you may obtain all your wishes for the world. O loving Mother, thank you for the gift that the world is on the brink of receiving!

Written by a Friend of
Medjugorje
June 1996

---

* Mirjana said it is something like the Rosary but is not the Rosary. Mirjana said, *"I say that because the prayers are continuous like the Rosary."* She circles her hand in describing this special prayer. It will be a new devotion that will enter the Church, like the Rosary, Scapular, Miraculous Medal and the Divine Mercy Chaplet. Once the prayers are released and the faithful begin praying them, it will help to cause a tsunami of conversion among nonbelievers around the world.

Through *Mirjana, A Mystery is Revealed,* and the above prayer, many, many prayer groups began to form, specifically for the purpose of praying for nonbelievers. A Friend of Medjugorje brought the Second of the Month out of the shadows, for countless followers of Our Lady. An awareness of the importance of the Second of the Month began to grow and prayers for nonbelievers began to increase. But, re-look at the *Prayer for Nonbelievers* more closely. Look how a Friend of Medjugorje ended the prayer. He wrote, *"O loving Mother, thank you for the gift that the world is on the brink of receiving!"* He was anticipating the gift of the prayer being released, yet something else happened instead, something much greater than the release of the prayer. Something that was a precursor of the release of the prayer.

Four months after the release of *Mirjana, A Mystery is Revealed* (in the July/September 1996 Newsletter), on January 2, 1997, a dramatic

and unexpected change happened with Our Lady.
Out of the blue, with no warning, Our Lady gave
a definitive time that She would be appearing to
Mirjana on the next Second of the Month, February
2, 1997, and an invitation for people to join Her if
they would like. This was incredible news and the
cause of both wonder and excitement. A Friend
of Medjugorje, upon receiving this news, immediately put out the first widespread call for people
to pray at the same time that Our Lady would be
praying with Mirjana for nonbelievers. A Friend of
Medjugorje wrote in the December 1996/February
1997 Caritas Newsletter:

"Clearly Our Lady is inviting us to join
in praying for all nonbelievers around
the world and in union with Her. We,
therefore, strongly encourage an hour
or more of prayer on the second of
each month, corresponding to the
exact moment of Our Lady's visit to
Mirjana. We* believe that these visits
on the second of each month are of
special significance and to miss this
opportunity will be one in which many
will regret once Our Lady fully releas-
es these prayers…"

For anyone desiring to respond to this call,
it would mean rising up in the middle of the night,
depending on where they lived in the world, in

---

* The founder of Caritas, known as a Friend of Medjugorje, often says, "we" when
writing because Our Lady gave him a personal message through Medjugorje
visionary, Marija, to "live in humility." He, therefore, deflects away from self,
deferring to the Community, even though he was the only witness of, or partici-
pant in, important events concerning the apparitions of Our Lady in Medjugorje.
He is the sole founder of Caritas, and he grew the mission through following Our
Lady's messages, forming the Community of Caritas in the same way.

order to be praying at the same time Our Lady was appearing to Mirjana. A Friend of Medjugorje strongly encouraged people to get up in the middle of the night, and even to ask their priests to open up churches or give them the keys so people could gather together. Was that an extreme thing to ask? Not if you know the history of Medjugorje.

A Friend of Medjugorje knew of times Our Lady had asked for the prayer group in Medjugorje to go up Cross Mountain in the middle of the night. Also, he often cites the August 2, 1981 apparition when Our Lady told Marija to go to her family gumno, (a field where the wheat crop is harvested), at 2:00 AM. Not only Marija went, but also Mirjana, along with 40 other people. If that was the case, why would it not be pleasing to Our Lady for people across the world to be in union with Her in prayer at the exact moment She was appearing upon the earth in Medjugorje?

Another story that he told to many Caritas
pilgrims to inspire and challenge them to climb
the mountains while in Medjugorje, came through
visionary Marija. Marija recalled that in the early
years of the apparitions, on a very cold and blustery
evening, during her apparition, Our Lady asked
all the prayer group to climb Cross Mountain at
11:00 PM because She was in great need of their
sacrifice for a specific intention. A very strong icy-
cold wind was blowing, and it was raining. Making
their way up the mountain was treacherous because
of the strong wind. The rain caused the path to be
filled with slippery mud, and it was completely dark,
with no moonlight to guide them.

Marija climbed in a wool skirt and remembered how freezing cold everyone was. When the
group made it to the 12th station, Our Lady suddenly appeared to Marija and bade them to turn
around and go back home. Their sacrifice was
sufficient to give Our Lady what She desired. She

then thanked everyone for their sacrifice. An extraordinary special grace was given for this heroic response to Our Lady's request, directly from Our Lady Herself. Everyone in the group actually heard Our Lady say **"thank you"** to them.*

Going back to a Friend of Medjugorje's call to hold a nightly vigil, in union with Our Lady, many answered the call with enthusiasm. The believers convinced many priests to come and participate in this vigil prayer. We learned later that many priests experienced profound conversion in seeing the fervent prayer of the Medjugorje followers. There was never any question why the gatherings were taking place—they were all for the purpose of

---

* Yet another story involved Jelena, one of the young girls who received inner locutions from Our Lady, who told the story to a Friend of Medjugorje. She and her prayer group were requested by Our Lady to go up Cross Mountain late at night, and they were told not to bring a flashlight. It was also a school night, and they were all expected to be in school the next morning, while only getting a few hours sleep. It is extremely dark on Cross Mountain; for many it would be unimaginable how one could get down the mountain in the complete dark. There are still more stories of the visionaries spending all night in Adoration, having no sleep, and arriving home at dawn to prepare for a busy day ahead of them. On the 20th anniversary of Our Lady's apparitions, as a special grace to Her visionaries, Our Lady began to reminisce with them of the many sacrifices they had made for Her in those beginning days. Joking a bit with Marija, Our Lady reminded Marija of all the sleep she got in those early years, when in reality, the visionaries got very little sleep.

praying for the souls of nonbelievers, in union with
Our Lady during Her February 2, 1997 apparition
to Mirjana, a Friend of Medjugorje continued in the
December 1996/February 1997 Caritas Newsletter:

> "We are privileged to even know about
> Heaven's plans and much more so to
> be able to actually participate in them.
> Go to all night adoration at that hour.
> Ask your priest to open your church to
> pray the Rosary at that hour. Gather
> your prayer group. Do whatever you
> are inspired to do, but please do not
> miss a glorious privilege to join and
> help Our Lady."

Again, a Friend of Medjugorje knew that for
many, it would be a sacrifice to get up in the middle
of the night and pray with Our Lady, so, he included
in the December 1996/February 1997 *Caritas Newsletter* a note to encourage them:

"These are wonderful times, and as Our Lady says, **'particular times.'** Surely, we are living what St. Louis de Montfort wrote of four hundred years ago, that the Virgin Mary would rise up apostles of the latter days and they would be given rule over the impious. Our Lady said on October 25, 1993:

> **'I invite you to become apostles of love.'**

"It requires love to rise up and pray in the night for those people who despise, even hate God. However, it separates the wheat from the chaff, the apostles from the regular men. You are invited by Our Lady Herself to be an apostle..."

A Friend of Medjugorje wanted to raise the people's spirits above the flesh so that they could respond to Our Lady's invitation with love. The response to a Friend of Medjugorje's call to prayer on the Second of the Month was like a wildfire spreading. What he wrote about doing in the December 1996/February 1997 Caritas Newsletter, is exactly what happened. People, in every part of the world, either alone, or with their families or prayer groups, prayed at the moment that Our Lady was with Mirjana on February 2, 1997. People wrote to us saying that their priests opened their churches so people could pray. One woman from Puerto Rico said that her church was full and several other churches throughout Puerto Rico were opened and also full. A letter from Reno, Nevada, sums up the spirit of the people who were praying because of a Friend of Medjugorje's call to pray with Our Lady on February 2, 1997:

*"Sunday at 2:00 AM, seventy people, includ-
ing two priests and a seminarian, gathered at
the church to pray the Rosary. Everyone was
so exhilarated! No one felt tired. Had we
thought before arriving that our presence was
a sacrifice because of the early hour, no such
thought remained. What a great privilege and
joy to be allowed to pray with Our Mother.
We also know that many people set their
alarms at home to rise and pray with us."*

One woman sent a fax to Caritas and said
that she had just found out about this special prayer
vigil on January 31, at 10:30 PM, just one day's
notice. She immediately called her priest, who was
already in bed, and asked him if he would open the
church at 5:00 AM on February 2. The priest said
yes right away. The next day, the woman was in-
terviewed on Catholic radio and invited people to
come and pray. The morning of February 2, 1997,
the church was full at 5:00 AM. From 5:00-7:00 AM,

they had Exposition of the Blessed Sacrament, sang
and prayed the Rosary. The woman wrote to us:

> *"The whole two hours seemed like 15 min-*
> *utes. It would be wonderful if we could pray*
> *together like this once a month (on the second*
> *of the month). Everyone was happy that they*
> *could respond to Our Blessed Mother's call*
> *for prayer for the unbelievers."*

Another person from Florida wrote:

February 4, 1997

> *"We did pray together from 5-8:00 AM on*
> *February 2, 1997. In fact, we spread the mes-*
> *sage and were accompanied (in spirit through*
> *distance) by at least 100 others – seventy of*
> *which were Polish nuns in Krakow, Poland.*
> *Of course, their time was the same as Croatia.*
> *We called them with the information. They*
> *also received the information with joy."*

Palm Coast, Florida

We received a letter from Argentina that said:

March 23, 1997

*"...we decided to respond on February 2nd by making a mini-pilgrimage to San Nicolas... February 2nd dawned a magnificently crisp clear and cool day (rare here, as we are in mid-summer on that date in the southern hemisphere)... Roads in Argentina are not exactly the greatest, but we were hoping and praying to be able to pull off the road at about 6:50 AM at some nice spot where we could all gather and pray together as 7:00 AM approached. Precisely at 6:50 AM, a beautifully paved crescent shaped turn-off presented itself to us on the right-hand side of the road. We all proceeded to pull off and exit our car. A powerful current of wind was blowing ('**I come in the wind!'** – Our Lady's words recalled) and the sky was magnificent..."*

Buenos Aires, Argentina

Some were saddened that so few people were going to hear about this special opportunity to be in prayer with Our Lady, knowing only a few Medjugorje followers. But when February 2, 1997 arrived, they ended up being deeply moved, as the following testimony shows:

February 3, 1997

"Upon receiving your special notice that a Friend of Medjugorje sent regarding the February 2nd time Our Lady was to appear, I called my sister, who I keep abreast of everything, and we decided to meet at a perpetual Adoration Chapel in the next town at 5:00 AM that morning. I belong to no prayer groups or anything, and my own parish priests are reluctant to acknowledge Medjugorje. As I was driving to the chapel, I thought how sad it was that my sister and I and possibly one or two others would be the only ones to pray in this small chapel; to share this great gift of Our

Lady's. As I drove, I noticed other cars on the road, and I was wondering if they were going to work. As I got closer to the chapel, I realized we were all going in the same direction, and as I pulled into the parking lot, there were many cars there and many others still coming. By the time 5:00 AM struck, the small chapel, which holds almost 60 people, was full and that parish's priest came to lead us in song and the Rosary and the Chaplet of Divine Mercy. We all prayed for nonbelievers together. I write this to let you know that your love and sacrifices for your God and for your people are worth all your efforts. I pray for you and thank you."

Turners Falls, Massachusetts

We are barely scratching the surface of letters, faxes and phone calls which were received in the days following February 2, 1997. Thousands had participated around the world in this prayer vigil with Our Lady. We know some of you who are reading this now were among those who were part of this historic event 23 years ago. The stories told were very special, and the results were deeply profound. We were to learn, shortly after, that Our Lady, Herself, seemed to respond to the enthusiasm of those across the world who prayed with Her in spirit, by making a major change in the status of Mirjana's inner locutions. Mirjana gave the happy news after her apparition on February 2, 1997:

> *"Please tell everyone that Our Lady's apparitions to me on the second of the month will now be like the regular apparitions to Vicka, Ivan, Jakov, and Marija. Our Lady said that whoever wants to be present at that apparitions can come. Our Lady said that much prayer is needed for those who have not yet come to know the love of God. This is all."*

Needless to say, this was a response from Our Lady that was beyond expectation. Walking through this chain of events, step by step, we see:

- First, we had the "intel drop" from a Friend of Medjugorje, sharing about the secret prayer that Mirjana prays with Our Lady, and exposing people to Our Lady's desire for everyone to pray for nonbelievers through his writing in the July-September 1996 Caritas Newsletter, entitled *Mirjana, A Mystery is Revealed*.

- Many responded to a Friend of Medjugorje's invitation to start prayer groups and to include the *Prayer for Nonbelievers* in their time of prayer.

- Just four months after the release of a Friend of Medjugorje's writing, *Mirjana, A Mystery is Revealed*, a break in the routine of Mirjana's meetings with Our Lady takes place. On January 2, 1997, Our Lady told Mirjana in the following month, on February 2, 1997, She would

appeal to Mirjana in an apparition and gave a
specific time for the apparition. Our Lady asked
Mirjana to make this public— and let people
know that She was inviting them to come and be
present for the apparition.

• A Friend of Medjugorje reacted to this news
  by calling upon Our Lady's followers to pray in
  union with Our Lady, at the same time around
  the world, encouraging people to even get up
  in the middle of the night to join in this great
  prayer event.

• Which, in turn, was followed by Our Lady
  choosing to replace Mirjana's Second of the
  Month inner locutions with actual apparitions
  and then inviting Her followers to come to be in
  Her presence!

  *"O loving Mother, thank you for the gift that
  the world is on the brink of receiving."*

Our Lady was moving ahead with Her plan. A Friend of Medjugorje observed from all of this that it was almost as if Our Lady was testing the water through this prayer invitation. She was once asked by the visionaries how long She would stay. Our Lady responded to their question:

June 29, 1981

> **"As long as you will want me to, my angels."**

Did the prayer vigils around the world influence God's decision to initiate the grace of sending Our Lady in apparitions to Mirjana on the Second of the Month—especially those who joined at 2:00 AM, 3:00 AM, 4:00 AM, 5:00 AM, with many in churches before the Blessed Sacrament in Adoration? Had this been a test to see if the world still "wanted" Our Lady, after 16 years of daily apparitions? It cannot be denied that it had an effect, and certainly Our Lady was pleased to see such devotion from thousands who participated in this *Prayer for Nonbelievers.* Those who participated in the vigils on February 2, 1997, testified how they were unexpectedly filled with great joy during the Holy Hour and experienced profound prayer. There was story after story, sent into Caritas, expressing to the founder (a Friend of Medjugorje) the many graces received by so many. They felt the presence of Our Lady and they felt the power of the unified prayer. Many people experienced conversion. Members of the Caritas Community were also in prayer at 3:00

AM, gathered in the Bedroom of Apparitions,* with the wife of a Friend of Medjugorje, who was just a week away from giving birth to their seventh child. Despite the early hour, the prayer was strong and profound.

"The hour at 4 AM [the time Mirjana had her apparition] *was one of the most blessed prayer times I have ever experienced. I know Our Lady's graces were being poured out then. Thank you for the leap of faith in alerting us."*

Tuscaloosa, Alabama

February, 1997

CHAPTER TWO

Extinguish the Flames

T here in the Bedroom of Apparitions, in the early morning hours of February 2, 1997, none of us could imagine that a great storm was brewing to viciously attack our founder, (a Friend of Medjugorje), and the mission of Caritas of Birmingham. Not everyone was pleased with this spontaneous prayer vigil gathering. In fact, the storm was about to boil over before there was any warning signs given of an impending storm. But before we continue on into this chapter, which will lay out what happened next, it is important to establish a few facts.

1. A Friend of Medjugorje never wrote or insinuated that anyone was **required** to get up and pray in the middle of the night.

2. A Friend of Medjugorje never wrote or insinuated that Our Lady or Mirjana had made a direct request for people to get up in the middle of the night to pray.

3. A Friend of Medjugorje **never** wrote or insinuated that Our Lady was going to be releasing a secret.

4. A Friend of Medjugorje made it perfectly clear that the prayer gathering was for one purpose only: to pray in union with Our Lady for nonbelievers and, in gratitude, for Our Lady allowing us to join Her at this time while She appears to Mirjana.

5. Among those associated with Caritas' mission, there was no confusion, no fear and no agitation, though thousands were phoning in and writing. There was *only* enthusiasm and

gratitude for having been contacted in time
to be able to participate.

6. There were many Medjugorje centers and
    followers of Our Lady, around the world,
    who were spreading the news about Mir-
    jana's February 2, 1997 apparition. It was
    big news in the Medjugorje world and there
    was very little time to spread the news before
    the day would arrive. Knowing this, a Friend
    of Medjugorje reacted quickly to the news.
    Having had the grace of interviewing Mirjana
    ten months earlier, learning of the secret
    prayer Our Lady taught her, having written
    about it in a newsletter and then a prayer to
    help break open the news to the world, read-
    ing hundreds of enthusiastic letters from his
    writing over several months, and then seeing
    Our Lady suddenly make a change, fueled
    his desire to ACT. He was in a totally differ-
    ent posture than most of those around the

world—his was a posture of anticipation, and he didn't want to fail Our Lady in rallying the troops when She led him to send out a call through the voice Our Lady had given him. This, perhaps, explains a little of how his own reaction differed so much from others who were responsible for informing Our Lady's followers of any changes in the apparitions. In regard to February 2, 1997, following Our Lady's messages and inspirations, he had built the infrastructure to rapidly react, striking quickly, to respond to Our Lady's call, even before others understood what Our Lady was revealing. Our Lady has used him to define many things concerning Medjugorje and its purpose, now, and in the future. He knew more and so was more responsible.

A Friend of Medjugorje says that Our Lady always sees what we give to Her and She responds beyond what we deserve or can even imagine.

His very history with Our Lady shows this, as was shown in the previous chapter. He has maintained, from the beginning of his involvement with Our Lady's apparitions, that whatever Our Lady shows him to say or do, he will make every effort to get the information to the masses. This has cost him a lot of persecution. It is important, at this point, to remember Our Lady's words:

July 25, 1999

> **"…pray and rejoice over everything that God does here, despite that satan provokes quarrels and unrest…"**

God does many things worth rejoicing over. But there was no way that satan would allow people all over the world to be making the sacrifice of getting up in the middle of the night in order to pray with Our Lady for nonbelievers. There was too much at stake for him to lose. In this case, satan did exactly what he normally does: he sowed division and confusion.

A Friend of Medjugorje made plans to be in
Medjugorje for Mirjana's February 2 apparition,
but felt a strong pull to spend several days in Rome
beforehand, in prayer and fasting. Spending most
of his time in St. Peter's Basilica, through a series of
small miracles, a letter from a Friend of Medjugorje
found its way into the hands of Pope John Paul II's
secretary, Fr. Stanisław Dziwisz, and he was invited
to attend the Pope's private Mass the morning of
January 30.

A Friend of Medjugorje was asked by the
Pope's secretary to do both the reading and the
responsorial psalm at the Mass, where he stood less
than five feet in front of the Holy Father. After the
Mass, a Friend of Medjugorje spent some time with
Pope John Paul II. The secretary introduced him
as the founder of a mission from Alabama that is
spreading the messages of Medjugorje. This immediately got the Pope's attention and as the secretary
continued to explain about the work of his mission,

his family and the Community, the Pope began giving blessings upon him—one for himself, a second for his

family and a third for the Community—three blessings. John Paul then accepted a copy of a Friend of Medjugorje's book, Words from Heaven, the Messages of Our Lady of Medjugorje.

This unexpected

A Friend of Medjugorje and Pope John Paul II, January 30, 1997.

Pope John Paul II, was known to have been a believer in Medjugorje. A Friend of Medjugorje gave Pope John Paul II a copy of Words from Heaven, and the Pope then questioned him about Medjugorje and his work. The Pope expressed to a Friend of Medjugorje about his interest in the "Bible Belt" of the United States, and that he has it in his heart to visit a Marian Shrine and the South. He was very well disposed to a Friend of Medjugorje. The Holy Father told him, *"I give you a blessing,"* making the Sign of the Cross on his forehead. Then he placed his hands on a Friend of Medjugorje's head and gave a blessing, saying, "This is for your family." When they finished, the Holy Father began to leave, then he stopped and turned around and said he wanted to give a blessing on the Community. A Friend of Medjugorje dropped to his knees and the Holy Father spread his arms out over a Friend of Medjugorje and imparted a prayer and a blessing over the Caritas Community.

meeting with the Holy Father set afire the heart
of a Friend of Medjugorje, and he was filled with
anticipation in arriving in Medjugorje the following day, January 31, 1997. That afternoon he went
to see Mirjana. He told her of the notice Caritas
had sent out, calling for people to join Our Lady in
prayer on February 2, and how great the enthusiasm was from people around the world in responding to that call.

Mirjana was happy to see a Friend of
Medjugorje and invited him to come to the apparition, telling him to arrive an hour early. He spent
the next day in prayer, thinking only of being with
Our Lady in the apparition the next morning and
being able to present to Her, in person, all those
who would be gathered around the world in prayer
during that time, oblivious to the fact that satan was
setting up a firestorm of hatred against him that
would manifest before Our Lady's apparition.

Medjugorje is seven hours ahead of Alabama time. Towards the end of the day of February 1, at Caritas in Alabama, it was learned that a deviously written fax was sent to all the Medjugorje centers, attacking a Friend of Medjugorje, not by name, but by description. There was no doubt who was being referred to in the fax that was filled with falsehoods and misleading statements.

A religious living in Medjugorje had gone to Mirjana and had expressed to her that a Friend of Medjugorje had caused great confusion, panic and fear among people, among other false allegations. Confusion? Panic? Fear? This was not at all the experience of the Community members who had been manning the phones and opening the mail over the past several weeks, after the announcement had been made. Mirjana was told that a Friend of Medjugorje was spreading fear about the secrets. Yet, reviewing what he wrote, there was no talk of the secrets, but only of prayer for nonbelievers.

It wasn't until the following morning, the
morning of February 2, that a Friend of Medjugorje
was informed of the attack upon him. He learned
of it just before going over to Mirjana's for the
apparition. Keep in mind that as this was evolv-
ing, the tens of thousands around the world were
together in prayer, in anticipation of Our Lady's apparition. Keep in mind, the great graces that were
being given to them all at this same time. Keep in
mind there were many promoters of Medjugorje
who were very jealous of the success of a Friend of
Medjugorje's mission and growing influence and
many jumped in on aligning against him. Following
is one of the faxed statements that were spread to
all the Medjugorje centers, while this beautiful out-
pouring of love for nonbelievers was being raised to
Heaven to greet Our Lady when She descended to
earth in Medjugorje. satan's fury had been raised
up to create damage control because of the many
conversions that would come from this event.

UPDATE ON THE FEBRUARY 2 APPARITION
OF BLESSED VIRGIN MARY TO MIRJANA.

(Following information received 2/2/97 from   )

Mirjana feels sorry because in the US a big wave of agitation and unrest is spreading due to a wrong interpretation of this event. This morning, she told me that we would only focus on what Our Lady simply said: It will be a normal apparition, she wants to open this meeting to everyone, as she needs us to pray for unbelievers. Mirjana clearly stated that the Gospa had **not mentioned anything connected to the secrets** on this occasion. She didn't let us assume **that they will be revealed soon** (same case of the 5 other visionaries: there is nothing new about the date of the secrets). **Any connection between this new type of prayer meeting and the secrets is only sheer human imagination!** Mirjana always insists on the fact that Our Lady wants us to pray rather than speak about the secrets. We only know that choosing this date - the 2nd day of the month - is relevant for the Blessed Mother. The hour of the apparition (11am) is just a convenient time for us here. For those who live far away, this hour might fall at night. The most important thing is not to gather at the same hour as in Medjugorje, but that everyone should be able to join. Better be many during the day than a few in the middle of the night! (The Gospa will be more concerned by our hearts than by clocks). If Mirjana lived in the States, Our Lady would visit her at day time and not at night, I guess. Vis-A-vis the clergy, its's important that the groups of Medjugorje witness much calm and solid common sense!

Note: This rather confirms the FAX issued by the   on Friday, Jan 31. which encouraged everyone to continue praying and to **LIVE OUR LADY'S DAILY MESSAGES!**

May Our Lord and Savior Jesus Christ continue to allow our Holy Mother Mary to be with us and may we answer Her pleas by responding to Her call.

A wrong interpretation of the event? Was it not to gather to pray for nonbelievers? Was the invitation not made by Our Lady to join Her, in Her presence? Where then is the wrong interpretation? Why would this be a problem for anyone?

1. The letter above, sent out on **February 2, 1997**, spreading the false information, says that Mirjana said:

    "She (Our Lady) wants to open this meeting to everyone, as She needs us to pray for unbelievers."

    A Friend of Medjugorje wrote in the **December 1996/February 1997** Caritas Newsletter:

    "Clearly Our Lady is inviting us to join in praying for all nonbelievers…"

2. The letter above, written by the religious on **February 2, 1997** states:

*"Mirjana clearly stated the Gospa had not mentioned anything connected to the secrets [You will read on down that this statement is taken out of context]...She didn't let us assume **they [the secrets] would be released soon.**"*

In the *Prayer for Nonbelievers*, written in June 1996 by a Friend of Medjugorje, it states:

*"We will pray that the dam of love, of God's mercy, will break forth, that your **new prayer be released 'soon'.**"*

A Friend of Medjugorje is asking that the new prayer for the conversion of nonbelievers be released soon. The *Prayer for Nonbelievers* does not refer to nor mention the secrets. However, revealed in the first volume of The Poem of the Man-God, books which Our Lady encouraged the faithful to read, it is interesting to note, as a young girl in the Temple, Our Lady prayed earnestly that God would shorten

the time and send the promised Messiah **'soon.'**
The *Prayer for Nonbelievers*, written by a Friend of
Medjugorje, asking for the conversion of nonbelievers
and the quick release of the prayer for them, is remi-
niscent of Our Lady's own prayer for the coming of
the Messiah 2,000 years ago.

3. The religious author (not Mirjana) of the letter above, written February 2, 1997 states:

   > *"Any connection between this new type
   > of prayer meeting and the secrets is **only
   > sheer human imagination**."*

   As revealed in *Mirjana, A Mystery is Revealed*, published in 1996, in a personal interview
with Mirjana, a Friend of Medjugorje asked her
what prayers she prays with Our Lady on the second of each month. Mirjana herself stated:

> *"Special prayers. **They are connected to the
> secrets!** They are prayed for nonbelievers or
> people who do not know the love of God…*

they are connected to the secrets. *Mirjana added, "But they are not the secrets."*

A Friend of Medjugorje states, *"It is obvious Medjugorje is connected to the secrets. The visionaries are connected to the secrets. Apparition Mountain is connected to the secrets. The letter of the religious caused damaging confusion."*

Is Mirjana **"imagining"** the connection between this new prayer and the secrets?

4. The author (not Mirjana) of the letter above, written February 2, 1997 states:

  "Mirjana insists that Our Lady wants us to pray rather than speak about the secrets."

Then why, over the decades, do the visionaries, including Mirjana, make it known to the people when Our Lady speaks to them of the secrets? Why not leave this detail out?

December 26, 1982

This is information which Mirjana gave to Father Tomislav Vlasic on November 5, 1983. He conveyed this information to the Pope on December 16, 1983. Father Vlasic's letter was published in "Is the Virgin Mary Appearing at Medjugorje?" (Paris, 1984), with this introduction:

> *During the apparition of December 25, 1982, according to Mirjana, the Madonna confided to her the tenth and last secret, and revealed to her, the dates in which the different secrets will be realized... The ninth and tenth secrets are serious. They concern chastisement for the sins of the world..."*

June 25, 1989

In Ivanka's Annual Apparition which lasted approximately eight minutes in all...Our Lady spoke about the fifth secret.

December 25, 2010

The following is Jakov's description of the apparition:

Our Lady spoke to me about the secrets and at the end said:

"Pray, pray, pray."

Additionally, Our Lady, Herself, stated to Mirjana on January 28, 1987:

"...Concerning the secrets...these are not known by the people. But when they learn of them, it will be too late... I would dearly wish that the Lord would permit me to enlighten you a little more on these secrets..."

While God has not permitted Our Lady to reveal to the world what the secrets are, God desires to make it known that there are secrets coming. In the Old Testament, before God brought down admonitions or chastisements to His people, it is written that He sent His prophets to warn the people. Jeremiah, Jonah and other prophets were to, **"Proclaim it in the streets."**

5. The author (not Mirjana) of the letter above, written February 2, 1997 states:

    "The most important thing is not to gather at the same hour as in Medjugorje, but that everyone should be able to join."

A Friend of Medjugorje wrote in the **December 1996/February 1997** Caritas Newsletter:

"We are privileged to even know about Heaven's plans and much more so to be able to actually participate in them…Do whatever you are inspired to do…These are particular times…It requires love to rise up and pray in the night…"

And to date, as Mirjana's Second of the Month apparitions have ended, there is a continued call, that was established 23 years ago, for everyone to gather together in prayer **at one time** on the second of each month.

In the fax above, it states, *"If Mirjana lived in the States, Our Lady would visit her at day time, and not at night, I guess."* How would anyone know that? Medjugorje visionary Marija has been at Caritas many times over the years and Our Lady has appeared as late as 11:30 PM. In Medjugorje, on the Mountain, Ivan often has had apparitions at 10:30 or 11:00 PM. Many pilgrims don't get to bed until 1:00 to 3:00 AM by the time they make it down from the mountain. Why was the fact that many people were getting up in the middle of the night to be in prayer with Our Lady being put in such a negative light?

Our Lady of Medjugorje said in 1993:

> **"...many who have an impassioned**
> **faith will cool off..."**

A Friend of Medjugorje, in his experience
with Our Lady and in dealing with souls, has seen
that many times, if satan cannot get people to lose
their belief, it is sufficient for satan to get people to
lose their enthusiasm. Something new, something
fresh often serves to enkindle enthusiasm, as what
was happening to thousands around the world.
What a travesty that water was going to be thrown
on the fire of conversion with the excuse for the
need of *"calm and solid common sense."* In a private meeting at the Vatican, a Friend of Medjugorje
was once told by Cardinal Emilio Trujillo, head of
the Pontifical Counsel of the Family, that there are
many good people doing bad things. The above
faxed statement was just the beginning. That same
day, another statement came out from another religious:

"We write in order to avoid the spreading of rumors like those that were recently spread in a sensational way to many Medjugorje prayer groups and caused much confusion and ' <u>inconvenience</u>.'"

These letters were printed and re-printed in numerous Medjugorje publications across the world. Needless to say, these letters caused great confusion in the Medjugorje world, in the hearts of believers, and a dampening of fervor in those who were already shaky in their commitment. Mirjana was approached by other Medjugorje people and told that a Friend of Medjugorje was causing confusion and agitation. Looking back 23 years later, we do not deny that there was agitation caused – against the kingdom of darkness. Following is a letter that was posted in another Medjugorje publication that came through the Parish Office of Medjugorje:

Jesus, I trust in You!

FEBRUARY 1, 1997

Re: concerning the information about the alleged new developments in connection with Mirjana Soldo (Dragicevic).

Dear friends of Medjugorje!

This evening, I spoke with Mirjana and, from the conversation with her, I did not obtain the impression that there is anything new. According to her words, she prays in a special way on the second of every month. Until now, she has done this alone, and in the future she will pray in the presence of others. Furthermore, she says that she knows nothing about Our Lady revealing any secret on the second of February. She also confirms that she has not requested that people pray throughout the world before the Blessed Sacrament at the same time that she will be praying.

With this letter, furthermore, I openly proclaim that those who have spread this news no longer belong to the family of Medjugorje.

Our Information Center [via the Press Bulletin] regularly sends out news of happenings in Medjugorje and all important information about the visionaries. This is an occasion to deny attention to those who willfully and selfishly spread news of the happenings in Medjugorje.

****

With each new statement, facts became more distorted. A Friend of Medjugorje never wrote that the February 2, 1997 apparition had anything to do with the secrets. Nor did he insinuate that Mirjana or Our Lady asked for people to meet in churches before the Blessed Sacrament. Those who actually read what he wrote were in peace and not in a state of confusion or fear. They understood that it was an opportunity to do something for Our Lady, to join with people around the world to respond to Our Lady's gesture of opening up Mirjana's apparition with prayer.

As you will read below, the statement from the letter displays how the authority in Medjugorje believe it is "their" call that is to be responded to, regarding who can be part of Medjugorje.

"With this letter, furthermore, I openly proclaim that those who have spread this news **no longer belong to the family of Medjugorje.**"

Yet it is Our Lady Who is calling, not those who think they can choose who is in the circle or not in the circle to be favored. The statement "openly proclaimed" is made to publicly denounce a Friend of Medjugorje. What is the purpose of this statement? What might be the motivation? The letter continues and clearly reveals the motivation in the next two sentences. Read each sentence slowly.

> "***Our*** *Information Center regularly **sends out news of happenings in Medjugorje** and all-important information about the visionaries.*

> "*This is an occasion* [This is our opportunity] *to deny attention to* [to slander; to murder the reputation of and to kill the voice of] *those who willfully and selfishly spread **news of the happenings in Medjugorje*** [apart from our control and power and self-interests].

What does the Parish Office want? What do they do? They want to be the only ones who send out news of the happenings in Medjugorje and information about the visionaries. Anyone else who does is "selfishly" spreading the news of Medjugorje. Who is selfish?

The aim of the parish statement was to shame and ostracize a Friend of Medjugorje, and force him out of Medjugorje, along with breaking up these prayer meetings. However, many groups continued to hold vigil every Second of the Month because of what they felt in their hearts. They experienced peace and grace. They opposed those who were saying *"Do not get up at the same time of the apparitions to pray."* But for some, the enthusiasm and joy that they had felt and testified to was destroyed. The statement was to decimate the mission of Caritas through damaging a Friend of Medjugorje's credibility and reputation. Others were confused and didn't know whether to continue or not with these prayer vigils, as the following letter shows:

Hi!

I'm a field angel, and we have been praying at 4 a.m. on the 2nd — here in Illinois. We're encouraged people to only come to Church if they really want to (many elderly, with children, etc) but that our prayers would be united with theirs.

This letter was presented to me at our Marian Movement of Priests Cenacle the evening of the 2nd. We were in Church at 4 a.m. (17 of us). People are now somewhat confused & I suspect that Satan may have a hand in this assembly, but this is from Medjugorje.

Please comment — we are only praying in Church for non-believers, not secrets to be revealed, etc.

I'm looking forward to hearing from you — Thank You — God's Blessings in these difficult approaching times —

       Love
       Fran

       E. Dundee, IL 60118

The above letter typed out:

Hi! I'm a Field Angel, and we have been praying at 4:00 AM on the 2nd [of the month]—here in Illinois. We've encouraged

*people to only come to church if they really
want to (many elderly, with children, etc.), but
that our prayers would be united with theirs.
This letter* was presented to me at our Marian Movement of Priests Cenacle the evening
of the 2nd. We were in church at 4:00 AM (17
of us). People are now somewhat confused.
I suspect that satan may have a hand in this
possibly, but this is from Medjugorje. Please
comment—we are only praying in church for
nonbelievers, not secrets to be released, etc.
I'm looking forward to hearing from you.
Thank you. God's blessings in these difficult
approaching times.*

Fran, East Dundee, Illinois

The growing influence of a Friend of
Medjugorje was the foundation of the attacks.
Many jumped on the bandwagon to ban him
from Medjugorje. The letter, regarding talking to

* The letter from page 52.

Mirjana, was put out to check a Friend of Medjugorje's influence. It stated:

> **"I did not obtain the impression that**
> **there is anything new."**

Mirjana was receiving inner locutions and
Our Lady changed that to actual apparitions—and
that was nothing new? Our Lady wasn't coming
to Mirjana at any fixed time, but suddenly then
named a definite time for the apparition—and that
was nothing new? Mirjana's meetings were private, only for her, but suddenly Our Lady declared
that everyone could now attend them—and that
was nothing new? Nothing's changed? We know
why there has been a minimizing of the events of
the apparitions and that is all we will share about
that topic. Of course, we now know the February 2,
1997 apparition was the beginning of a huge plan of
Our Lady regarding the conversion of nonbelievers; that it was making way for the Second of the
Month messages with a unique character, different

from Marija's 25th of the month messages, and that the Second of the Month would become the biggest draw for pilgrims coming to Medjugorje for years.

A Friend of Medjugorje didn't have to know exactly what was behind Our Lady's actions on February 2, 1997, he only knew that everything Our Lady does is significant and has purpose and meaning. Therefore, we who follow Her, must respond however everyone is inspired to respond. A Friend of Medjugorje was attacked because he dared to be a voice defining Medjugorje. He had a unique understanding of Our Lady's messages, and many people were beginning to follow him. His growing following and influence had to be stopped, but he refused to allow Caritas of Birmingham to turn into a cookie cutter Medjugorje center. He knew from his own experience, and many others he had met over the years, that if any nail was standing up apart from the others, it was to be hammered down. But this was contrary to Our Lady's own words. Our

Lady wanted everyone to have the freedom to live
and spread Her messages as each was inspired to
do. In a Monthly Message given while Marija was
staying in the home of a Friend of Medjugorje and
his wife, Our Lady said:

November 25, 1988

> **"...I call you to prayer for you to have
> an encounter with God in prayer. God
> gives Himself to you, but <u>He wants
> you to answer in your own freedom to
> His invitation... Watch in vigil</u> so that
> every encounter in prayer be the joy of
> your contact with God..."**

This message is the perfect mirror of what
the February 2, 1997 prayer gathering was for
many people who participated in the night vigil.
**"...Watch in vigil so that every encounter in prayer
be the joy of your contact with God..."** While many

followed the lead of a Friend of Medjugorje, sadly others, many others, fell away.

Yet, for all that happened in those turbulent days of February 1997, Our Lady came on March 2, 1997, the following Second of the Month, and in an apparition to Mirjana spoke these words:

March 2, 1997

>**"Dear children, pray for your brothers who haven't experienced the love of the Father, for those whose only importance is life on earth. Open your hearts towards them and see in them my Son, who loves them. Be my light and illuminate all souls where darkness reigns. Thank you for having responded to my call."**

For those who had in their hearts only concern for earthly "inconvenience," Her words were a direct contradiction. For those against people getting up in the middle of the night to pray, in the darkness of night, Our Lady said, to **"Be my light… where darkness reigns."**

The controversy, which was created, not by a Friend of Medjugorje, but by those who made controversy out of his words, effectively stopped Our Lady. How was Our Lady stopped? In the end, they trusted themselves over Our Lady's plans. History now shows, that after March 2, 1997, Mirjana withdrew from the public once again. This was to become the last public Second of the Month message until January 2, 2000.

Many past apparitions had interference from the authorities who placed themselves over Our Lady. Fatima's miracle of the sun dancing and the muddy ground drying up was a much smaller miracle than what Our Lady was going to give. Why was the miracle not given in its fullness in Fatima? Our Lady revealed that it was because the authorities arrested the children.

A Friend of Medjugorje has relayed the following over and over through the years:

"Have we lost things Our Lady wanted to do in Medjugorje because of self-interest, seeking power, personal agendas? We can say yes. Our Lady has wanted much more than what Her visitation brings but often Our Lady's plans interfere with human plans. There are serious tragedies that have severely hurt Our Lady's wants and plans. But they won't be mentioned for the sake of Medjugorje and for the good not to be hurt."

"God bless you all! I'll be up at 4 a.m. to pray. Thank You!!!! You're making a saint out of me. The good you're doing will only be revealed to you in Heaven—don't give up— you've brought me from an evil, angry, house-wife to a peace-filled wife and mother. I'm a miracle. Thank you all."

Yorkville, Illinois

January, 1997

CHAPTER THREE

Missing the Messages

Those who have followed a Friend of Medjugorje's witness, translated through his writings from early on, know that he has given his life to the messages of Our Lady and their propagation. When many in the Medjugorje movement were more involved in organizing conferences and similar events, which served to introduce Medjugorje to many new people, as well as brought about conversions, Our Lady was, however, showing him that was not Her plan for him. While the conferences were fruitful and had merit, Our Lady was calling him to give his life to prayer and sacrifice to understand Our Lady's words and put them into life.

Once, in the late eighties, while in Medjugorje for five weeks, a Friend of Medjugorje went up Apparition Mountain and Cross Mountain every day, praying for one intention: the grace to understand Our Lady's messages. It was during this period of time that he began to see two different contradicting paths that Medjugorje believers were taking. One path, being propagated by many, believed Medjugorje was just another Fatima or another Lourdes.

Also, in this time, many were leaving Medjugorje to follow other supposed visionaries, placing Medjugorje in a line, side-by-side, no more or no less important than other visionaries who claimed to also have "a plan for the salvation of the world." There was a long period of time in which people had grown bored with Our Lady's "simple" messages from Medjugorje. It was common to hear Medjugorje priests and visiting priests say from the pulpit that all Our Lady was doing was simply repeating the Gospel, and that there was nothing new being said by Our Lady than what She had said in Her past apparitions. Messages from other alleged visionaries, in other locations around the world, were, on the contrary, full of apocalyptic warnings and coming chastisements, which drew people through their sensationalism. Today, most of those alleged visionaries have proven to be false voices and, when they faded away, many who had first followed Medjugorje never returned. The devil's tactic had been successful.

A Friend of Medjugorje never swayed from Medjugorje; he never gave his ear to other voices. For him, it went against common sense to think God needed to establish a hundred separate "plans to save the world,"* especially when often what it did was cause division in prayer groups over what "voice" to follow, while at the same time diluting

---

* A Friend of Medjugorje has always maintained that Our Lady "has many plans" through Medjugorje. Some small, some medium and some larger plans. Regarding "larger" plans, there are a very few select, major worldwide reaching plans.

Our Lady's voice from Medjugorje, the central command post established by God for the salvation of the whole world.

Our founder continuously called out warnings not to be swayed by "lying voices," and drew both praise and resentment for his stance; praise from those who appreciated someone willing to go against the current tide, to say what they discerned to be truth, and resentment from those who were putting all their investment into other alleged apparitions. In the end, many Medjugorje centers ended up closing, having lost their bearings, as they drifted further and further away from Medjugorje, the source of grace God had established from the beginning.

Meanwhile, under the leadership and strong conviction of a Friend of Medjugorje, Caritas of Birmingham kept growing and prospering. This happened despite constant attacks on him for daring to challenge ideas and beliefs that, while popular with many people, were really deceptions from the devil whose aim was to divert as many people as possible from the conversion waters of Medjugorje. But because a Friend of Medjugorje was never trying to win a popularity contest, and he was willing to weather the negative consequences that came to him for speaking unpopular truths, those who appreciated hearing the truth, even difficult truths, became loyal followers of Our Lady, through a Friend of Medjugorje, and these numbers continually were rising.

Regarding the messages of Our Lady of Medjugorje, reason, prayer, fasting and common sense gave clear discernment, leading a Friend of Medjugorje to believe that Our Lady would not be giving so many words and messages without a deeper meaning to them. While many today would not admit it, virtually everybody left the messages behind because they believed they had spiritually "outgrown" them, or they were too repetitive, or

they said nothing. A Friend of Medjugorje discerned differently. He prayed many years for Our
Lady to help him understand the "profoundness" of
the messages, as She said in an apparition to Marija
in his home:

December 4, 1988

> **"I invite you to live the profoundness**
> **of the messages that I give."**

His heart told him that Our Lady was here
for a reason, and She was giving words for a reason,
and in the message above Our Lady confirmed this
to him. Slowly, Our Lady began to show a Friend
of Medjugorje how to break open the messages
and unlock the beauty, wisdom and profoundness
contained within them. He started looking intently
at Our Lady's words and perceiving within them a
wealth of knowledge and inspiration that was different from what She had done through Lourdes or
Fatima. In fact, he saw that Our Lady was revealing

truth in a new way that She had never before expressed in Her other earlier apparitions.

While many were passing over Our Lady's words as insignificant, a Friend of Medjugorje was deeply struck by certain messages Our Lady had given, such as Her message of May 2, 1982, when She said:

> **"I have come to call the world to conversion for the last time. Afterwards, I will not appear any more on this earth."**

Or, when on August 2, 1981, Our Lady said:

> **"...A great struggle is about to unfold. A struggle between my Son and satan. Human souls are at stake..."**

The more a Friend of Medjugorje delved into Our Lady's messages, the more he recognized the purpose of Our Lady's coming. For instance, he

saw that Our Lady kept referring to a "plan" in Her
messages, but never revealed it. Our Lady would
say, **"pray for the plan,"** without giving any indica-
tion of what the plan was. A Friend of Medjugorje
prayed to understand what Our Lady's plan was.
Finally, on January 25, 1987, Our Lady revealed it:

> **"…I want you to comprehend that
> God has chosen each one of you, in
> order to use you in a great plan for the
> salvation of mankind. You are not able
> to comprehend how great your role is
> in God's design. Therefore, dear chil-
> dren, pray so that in prayer you may be
> able to comprehend what God's plan is
> in your regard. I am with you in order
> that you may be able to bring it about
> in all its fullness…"**

Our Lady confirmed to a Friend of
Medjugorje, that Medjugorje was indeed, different
and unique among all Her other apparitions.

Many today, who are entering into the Medjugorje world for the first time, come in with the understanding that the messages are important and that they should be paying attention to Our Lady's words. But, back in 1986 and into the early 1990's, there was little attention given to Our Lady's words. From the beginning of the apparitions, there was great excitement and great yearning for what Our Lady said. In time, it became routine. Then came a phase where only the committed villagers sought out the message. Many of them were the older people. Then the message went through long periods of little interest even to pilgrims.

As the mission of Caritas of Birmingham grew and, while a Friend of Medjugorje was forming the Community of Caritas, he deeply imprinted the importance of Our Lady's messages upon this mission and Community. Whenever Our Lady gave a new message, everything else stopped in the mission until the message was received, printed and sent out. And today, it is the same. Nothing else is more important than getting Our Lady's words out to the world. This remains the priority of a Friend of Medjugorje, and through him, the mission of Caritas.

The Founder of Caritas of Birmingham Before He Became Known as A Friend of Medjugorje

The founder of Caritas of Birmingham (a Friend of Medjugorje) initiated a practice early in his involvement with Medjugorje that has spread worldwide over the years. While promoting the messages is the priority of Caritas' mission, the foundation of our founder was and is to put the messages into his own personal life and family first, which is also how he formed the Community of Caritas. It is only then that one could promote and propagate the message. Thereby, it is something living and not just ink on paper. One's live witness brings the message to life in others. Being very practical in how he approached Our Lady's messages, he began to randomly pick a message to read and live each day, as Our Lady would later confirm:

December 25, 1989

> **"...little children, read everyday the messages I gave you and transform them into life...."**

His practice of picking a random message went back to the middle to upper 1980's. As he did this, he began to see that Our Lady was speaking to him through Her words and the circumstances of his life. He eventually brought this "way" into the mission and the Community of Caritas—while being inspired how to guide both through the inspirations Our Lady gave in Her words each day.

As his hunger for the messages grew, he began compiling the all the messages Our Lady had given to each visionary into a single book. Up to this point, at the end of the 1980's, there was no such resource available. In the year 1990, a Friend of Medjugorje published his first book, *Words from Heaven, the Messages of Our Lady from Medjugorje,* and has continually updated it throughout the decades. It is in its 19th edition and with every edition, several updates are made in the course of reprinting the book each year. It is the best and most complete message book available, by far, for Our Lady's messages in the world. It is the gold-standard for the messages. *Words from Heaven* became "the book" from which the messages were randomly chosen for each day in the Community.

Seeing success come through Our Lady's words chosen in this manner, he began to propa-

gate this "way" outside of the mission, but when
he did, he was ridiculed, mocked and slandered for
doing so. It was ridiculous, many said of him, for
expecting Our Lady to speak to someone through
randomly picking a message. So much resistance
came against him, so much ridicule with the purpose of making him out to be a simpleton for his
simple but strong faith in using this method to
discern God's will, that he prayed to Our Lady to
validate this "way" he believed She had led him to
discover. Within days of this prayer, he was looking for a book to read out of his library and picked
out a book on St. Francis. Opening up the book at
random, he was amazed to find the story of how St.
Francis' first convert became convinced that God
was calling him to join Francis in his way of life of
poverty:

> *Bernard, one of the wealthiest young men of*
> *Assisi, became intrigued by reports about one*
> *of his peers—Francesco di Bernardone, previ-*

*ously known as something of a dandy and ca-
rouser—who had recently aroused wonder, as
well as ridicule, by his ostentatious embrace of
poverty. His curiosity piqued, Bernard invited
Francis to dine with him and spend the night
in his home.*

*During the course of the night, Bernard was
so moved by the sound of Francis' ardent
prayers that he confronted Francis the next
day and asked his help in discerning God's
will. Opening the missal at random, Francis
alighted on the text, "If you wish to be perfect, go and sell all you own, and give it to the
poor." A second time he opened [Scripture]
and found, "Take nothing for your journey."
On a third attempt [again, opening up Scripture at random], he found, "If anyone would
follow me, let him deny himself." "This is the
advice that the Lord has given us," Francis
proclaimed. "Go and do as you have heard."*

Taking these instructions to heart, Bernard disposed of his property and adopted Francis's way of life.

Undaunted by the persecution, especially after reading about St. Francis, our founder continued to place the messages in a primary position of importance. Through his commitment of constantly lifting the messages up out of obscurity and pointing to them as essential, not only in understanding the purpose of why Our Lady is coming to Medjugorje, but essential in living the new life Our Lady is calling everyone to, he started a revolution of the messages, showing that the messages were not mundane, but filled with deep meaning. Now, 34 years later, the messages of Our Lady are seen as having an important part in Our Lady's plan. It is hard to believe, for anyone who has joined the Medjugorje world in the past 10-15 years, that there was a time when Our Lady's messages were not only seen as unimportant, but, were suppressed or minimized. Many today may find that hard to believe, but that was exactly the case.

History of the Second of the Month Apparitions

A Friend of Medjugorje often urges us to meditate on the time when the messages will stop, when the apparitions will end, in order to lead us to become more fervent in the time we still have with Our Lady. Yet, even so, we know we will all be shocked when Our Lady's apparitions end. We were all given a preview of this when Mirjana's Second of the Month apparitions ended on March 18, 2020. A Friend of Medjugorje was just as shocked and saddened as everyone else. Looking at the history of the messages Our Lady gave on the Second of the Month, this is what we know:

- On January 2, 1997, Our Lady announced
  Mirjana would receive an apparition on February 2, 1997, instead of an inner locution. On
  February 2, 1997, Our Lady changed this perma-
  nently. From this day, Mirjana began receiving
  regular apparitions of Our Lady on the second
  of every month. On March 2, 1997, when Our
  Lady appeared, She gave **the first message** on
  the day of prayer for nonbelievers.

- But after March 2, 1997 until January 2, 2000
  there is no public record of Our Lady giving a
  message to Mirjana in her Second of the Month
  apparitions. We are not sure if Our Lady did
  not give messages, or if they simply were not
  made public. Many people who were following a Friend of Medjugorje's writings through
  the Caritas Newsletters were contacting Caritas,
  wanting to know more about praying for nonbelievers, but there was no information to pass
  along. Then suddenly, on January 2, 2000, at the

turn of the new millennium, Our Lady came with a heartfelt cry to Her children:

January 2, 2000

> **"Never as much as today, my heart is begging for your help! I, your Mother, am begging my children that they help me to realize what the Father has sent me for. He has sent me among you because His love is great. At this great and holy time in which you have entered, pray in a special way for those that have not experienced yet the love of God. Pray and wait!"**

- After this plea and the words, **"pray and wait,"** Our Lady again went silent with no public record of any messages given in Her Second of the Month apparitions with Mirjana until October 2, 2002, followed by another gap.

- In 2003 and 2004, there were more messages
  with gaps between many of them, and sometimes Our Lady would appear but give no message. From 2005 to 2006, the messages of Our
  Lady through Mirjana were more regular, with
  fewer gaps between messages.

During all these years, it was very difficult to
get a hold of Our Lady's messages from the Second
of the Month apparitions, even if you were in the
village when the message was given. It was not un-
common to have to wait one day, two days, or even
longer to get Our Lady's Second of the Month message. We would have to turn away hundreds of dis-
appointed pilgrims from the Caritas Mission House
in Medjugorje without being able to give them the
message. "Come back tomorrow," we would say.
"But, we're leaving the village tonight," they would
respond. It was extremely frustrating and a cause
of indignation for a Friend of Medjugorje in seeing how Our Lady's words were being purposely

delayed. There were always people who were seen
to have the message in hand several hours after
the apparition, but for those not considered to be
"in the family of Medjugorje," such as a Friend of
Medjugorje and the Community members, Our
Lady's messages were often kept from them as long
as possible. Month after month it was the same. A
Friend of Medjugorje would direct Caritas Community members in Medjugorje to go hunt down
the message. Secret alliances had to be formed with
individuals in the village to "sneak" the message to
us. They did not want to be known as the one giving the message to Caritas because they were afraid
of being persecuted by "the powers that be" in
Medjugorje.

It was June 2006, when a Friend of
Medjugorje was in the village for the Anniversary
of Our Lady's apparitions that he had finally had
enough. Having lived through the same scenario
for years with Ivan's prayer group apparitions and

Medjugorje photo taken on Monday, October 2, 2006, at 9:11 AM.

When Mirjana's Second of the Month apparitions became public again, they were first taking place at a basketball court in front of Medjugorje visionary Marija's home. Then, the apparitions moved to a tent and then to a building at the Cenacolo. Thousands would stream in, often waiting in the street, all night long. It was difficult to get a place inside, and the location was not conducive to allowing pilgrims to be present, as many would end up outside. This picture was taken through the window of the Cenacolo building. Pilgrims can be seen crowding around Mirjana inside, as well as the reflection of many more pilgrims outside.

messages, he had taken it upon himself to set up an infrastructure to get Ivan's messages translated into English and then distributed through the Caritas Mission House in Medjugorje—the only place, now for decades, that the prayer group messages are made available for pilgrims. It was being said that Ivan's prayer group messages on the mountain were only meant for those who were present at the apparition, and therefore, they shouldn't be distributed to anyone who wasn't on the mountain. Yet, some of the most profound messages Our Lady has given over the years have been through Ivan's prayer group on the mountain. A Friend of Medjugorje knew this was a ruse to diminish Our Lady's messages. He defied those who suppressed Ivan's prayer group messages.

When every avenue became closed to him getting Ivan's messages, a Friend of Medjugorje instructed Caritas Community members to record Ivan when he relayed the message after the mountain apparitions and bring the recording to a translator who translated the message directly from the Croatian into English. From there, Community members went back to the Mission House the same night the message was given, printed the message on special message cards designed by a Friend of Medjugorje, and began distributing them FREE to pilgrims passing by the Mission House and on the streets of Medjugorje. Many times it was long after midnight before the Community members went home, which was not until the streets were empty. The reaction of pilgrims passing by was surprise and joy that they were receiving the message, shocked that they were receiving it so quickly, and humbly grateful they were receiving them for free.

Since this worked so successfully for Ivan's prayer group apparitions, a Friend of Medjugorje was undaunted in establishing the same infrastructure to get the Second of the Month messages out and distributed. But, as soon as a Friend of Medjugorje established a way to get Mirjana's messages into the hungry hands of pilgrims, circumventing the "circle" of those who did not have to wait for it, "the powers that be" suddenly decided to

make Mirjana's messages more easily available to
everyone in Medjugorje. The motivation to give it
to everyone happened only after many people started coming to the Caritas Mission House when they
learned they could get Mirjana's messages there.
Once the messages were finally being made available to "everyone," there wasn't a need for Community members to have to record it and get the
message translated. A Friend of Medjugorje said
it was a good thing that others took this over, since
the Caritas Community was not in Medjugorje during the winter months. He has often commended
those who work to get the message out, even if he
has sometimes publicly called them out for not being timely about it. On February 2, 2012, a Friend
of Medjugorje wrote, after there was a 9-hour delay
in getting the message, *February 2, 2012 Message
Not Released Don't Blame Us.* Here is a short ex-
cerpt from that writing:

"When a message date approaches, Caritas has preplanned who will be involved and where they will be. On the 2nd of the month in Medjugorje, we are preparing all night. At Caritas in Alabama, we have 4-6 people up at 3:00 a.m., preparing to receive the message, and working on the description and writing to get the message out immediately. It goes out on Medjugorje.com, put on our phone system, and goes out in print through our mailing list. When we are with Marija, no matter where in the world, plans have been made, even days in advance, to have the message immediately sent back to the parish office in 10-20 minutes, to give to the translators who are ready to go to work immediately, and from there a network of communities, Medjugorje Centers and other media programming receive it, who spread it to the whole world… Those responsible after receiving the message first are ir-

responsible in grasping what this delay causes
around the world... There was a snowstorm in
Medjugorje, but this does not excuse the delay
as contingent plans should always be in the
works for whatever happens. The mail runs,
despite snow or rain, and this message from
Heaven is too important for this laisse quasi
approach to get it out..."

Some in the Medjugorje movement, at the
time he wrote this, thought he was being a little
too hard, but, Caritas, being the largest Medjugorje
center in the world, was on the receiving end of the
phone calls from people rightfully demanding to get
the message.

In the timeline of Second of the Month apparitions, what we can now see from when a Friend of
Medjugorje set up an infrastructure to get the Second of the Month messages out, and when others
took this over, is that from 2007 onward, **Our Lady**
had words for us every month. Was it that Our

Medjugorje photo taken at the Blue Cross on Apparition Mountain, Friday, October 2, 2009 at 8:48 AM.

Once the apparitions moved to the Blue Cross, thousands were able to attend, and often spent the night on the mountain. This picture of Mirjana was taken by a Caritas Community member and is one of the more popular pictures taken of Mirjana on the Second of the Month. This picture has appeared and re-appeared in numerous Medjugorje websites and publications. This picture above is second only to the picture which was taken of Mirjana's eye, in which a reflection of the Cross and what appears to be a "woman" can be seen. More about this picture will be told in Chapter 4.

Lady saw a hunger for Her words and responded accordingly? If She did not give messages before, and was now giving them regularly every Second of the Month, one would be led to think so. Again, we do not know whether the missing messages were apparitions without messages, or whether Our Lady gave a message and it was never released publicly.

A Friend of Medjugorje has had several encounters with the messages being slowed down, suppressed and has sometimes seen efforts to stop them. satan hates Our Lady's messages and that should be enough to believe these words, that there has been serious efforts to stop the messages. A Friend of Medjugorje has been instrumental in many messages being released and preserved. If you are a pilgrim in Medjugorje, the Caritas Mission House is the only place today where you can receive the 25th of the month messages, the 2nd of the month messages, Ivan's prayer group messages, and the annual messages given to Ivanka, Jakov and Mirjana—**all free** for pilgrims on beautiful gold embossed keepsake cards.

Our Lady's plan continued to move forward with Her apparitions and messages to Mirjana on the second of every month, until Our Lady told her on March 18, 2020, that She would no longer appear to Her on the Second of the Month. It is sad to think that part of Medjugorje's history is over, but as Medjugorje has always been called and known as "Our Lady's School of Holiness"—every school education ends with a graduation. After graduation, every student is expected to take what he has learned and apply it in real life. It is up to all of us to take the lessons Our Lady has taught us over these many years to open the hearts of nonbelievers and lead them out of their darkness into the light and love that is waiting for them through coming to know Our Lady and Her Son.

"I was so excited to be able to be a part of this special time. My prayer hour was from 2-3 a.m. Sunday morning. I was concerned that I would sleep through and miss it. I was concerned that I would be too sleepy to pray very well...The most wonderful thing happened. I was able to set up my shrine by 1:50 a.m. I began my prayers then. I prayed all three mysteries of the Rosary, plus, after the Sorrowful Mysteries, the Chaplet of Mercy. I wasn't sleepy! I was too awake and aware I couldn't believe it...No one ever knew about it. My candle burned itself out at 3 a.m. I felt part of a worldwide prayer group joined to Our Lady as She and Mirjana prayed...Thank you for always being true to the message of Our Lady and for always staying focused on Medjugorje and its meaning."

San Diego, CA
February, 1997

CHAPTER FOUR

March 18...Trust the Plan

There are certain days in history that the dates will always be remembered, like September 11, 2001. The world was changed forever the day the World Trade Center towers came down. It holds a special place among the greatest events of history. Such, also, will be the case with March 18, 2020.

In his book, <u>Big Q, Little Q: The Calm Before the Storm</u>, released in early March 2019, **one year before Our Lady ended the Second of the Month apparitions** to Mirjana, a Friend of Medjugorje wrote:

> ...Every March 18th is significant because it is one year closer to the actual event of March 18th in the future. Each March 18th is a precursor, a sign of things to come...

How can this not be considered a prophetic statement! For on **March 18, 2020, one year later**, from the time a Friend of Medjugorje wrote these words, Our Lady stopped Her monthly apparitions to Mirjana. The Medjugorje world was in shock. The whole world was just entering the nightmare of what would become the worldwide coronavirus pandemic. U.S. President Donald Trump had stopped travel from Europe to the United States just days before March 18th. It was getting harder for U.S. citizens to get back into the United States. Italy was locked down because of the virus with many nations following suite. A Friend of Medjugorje spoke extensively about these circumstances on his March 18, 2020, *Radio Wave* broadcast entitled, *Why Did Our Lady Stop the Second of the Month Apparitions?* He said:

...Different events have happened during the 39 years [of Our Lady's apparitions], but this is much more shocking to people because the conditions in the world are speaking to us. The signs of the times are talking to us. It's like Nebuchadnezzar when the hand was writing on the wall. It can't be any clearer of what's taking place. So, people are scared right now. They're shaken by this. And in some ways, they're justified...

Many in the Medjugorje world will remember where they were and what they were doing when they heard the news that Our Lady stopped the Second of the Month apparitions. A Friend of Medjugorje explained in the March 18, 2020, broadcast that the events of the world were a perfect set up to get our attention, and gave a clearer explanation of Our Lady's plan, as it involved the Second of the Month apparitions. Not surprisingly, he didn't connect the coronavirus to the plans of Our Lady. The coronavirus is a crisis that will pass, but Our Lady's plans are eternal. He continues:

...So, in the hourglass of time, the sand has run out for the Second of the Month apparitions. Does that mean that we're at the end? No. It means it is a new beginning because this is the road map, this is the path, this is the book of twenty-three years of messages, a highway to convert and bring non-believers to Our Lady's Son through Our Lady. You have heard me talk about this many times. In the Second of the Month messages, Our Lady rarely says the name of Jesus... I saw long ago in the messages that Our Lady will say, 'my Son, my Son' because nonbelievers can accept Our Lady as a mother, easier than accepting "Jesus." But the Mother's "Son" can be accepted. It is part of Our Lady's **strategy**, how to open the hearts of people that have been hurt or turned off by a bad witness from Christians. Many Christians haven't been good witnesses. So, the name of Jesus is not an attraction for many people. But they are attracted to this Woman, the Mother, and through Her, they can accept Her Son. **This is the plan...**

A Friend of Medjugorje said that March 18 is a sign of things to come. It is part of the plan. He wrote in <u>Big Q, Little Q: The Calm Before the Storm</u>, that we are seeing manifest in the physical world, that which is happening in the spiritual world. The seemingly abrupt ending of the Second of the Month apparitions, is not without being part of a larger plan of

Heaven. How does it manifest, and for what purpose?
In Chapter 2, of <u>Big Q, Little Q, the Calm Before the
Storm</u>, a Friend of Medjugorje wrote:

> ...Medjugorje is Our Lady's Central
> Headquarters—the Pentagon—in
> this war against evil. Our Lady has to
> have both, Her actors—**those who are
> playing out certain significant roles
> within the events of our day,** and Her
> apostles—**those who are aligned with
> the Queen's plans to lead the world to
> conversion and salvation.** Not every-
> one involved in implementing Her
> plans are apostles of Our Lady. Some,
> like Trump, are actors—those who
> have a great role and are important to
> the success of Her plan. Her plan also
> includes those who, since their birth,
> have been groomed for their part

throughout their whole lives. They do not necessarily know Our Lady is behind what they are inspired to do, but they will find the strength within themselves to fight through to win this battle.

Our Lady has Her plans, through man, but She also has opposition.

July 12, 1984

> **"…These days satan wants to frustrate my plans. Pray that his plan not be realized…"**

There is a great battle going on, as we know from Our Lady's August 2, 1981, message:

> **"…A great struggle is about to unfold. A struggle between my**

**Son and satan. Human souls are
at stake."**

The spiritual realms of Heaven and
hell, which we can't see, are in battle,
but they fight their battle physically
through man. The actors guided by
Light and apostles of Our Lady are
on one side, and the actors guided by
darkness and demons of satan are on
the other side. The two sides have already begun to engage. The dark side
is going to be broadsided by the Light.

= End of Big Q, Little Q, the Calm Before the Storm, Quote =

So, here we are, in the midst of the
coronavirus pandemic, and Our Lady stops Her
Second of the Month apparitions. Do you feel lost?
A Friend of Medjugorje said that you will feel lost

if you do not understand Our Lady's plan. But, if one has been putting into practice Our Lady's instructions, and engaging in battle, one can see the plan at work.

To see the plan, let's "turn back the clock" one more time. Our Lady, *in Her first Second of the Month message* given on **March 2**, 1997 said:

> **"…Be my light and illuminate all souls where darkness reigns…"**

On March 2, 1997, the world was walking in darkness. Our Lady was calling us to be the light. Interestingly, coincidentally perhaps, in Our Lady's *last Second of the Month message*, which was also on a **March 2**, Our Lady said:

March 2, 2020

> **"…it is a time of vigil… Bring the light of my Son and <u>keep breaking the dark-</u>**

ness which all the more wants to seize
you. Do not be afraid..."

When is a vigil? You hold a vigil through the
night, awaiting morning. The plan is being revealed.
Our Lady's words above, in the last Second of the
Month message, **"...keep breaking the darkness..."**
was illuminated one year before, in March 2019,
when a Friend of Medjugorje wrote prophetically
that the darkness will be "broadsided by the Light"
in his book, Big Q, Little Q, the Calm Before the
Storm, published 12 months before Our Lady said,
"keep breaking the darkness." Our Lady, in Her
Second of the Month apparitions has and continues
to be bringing us from dark to Light. We are in the
vigil awaiting dawn. It is the plan. Trust the plan.

This picture was taken of Mirjana, September 2, 2011, 8:46 AM. Look carefully at the eye to the left.

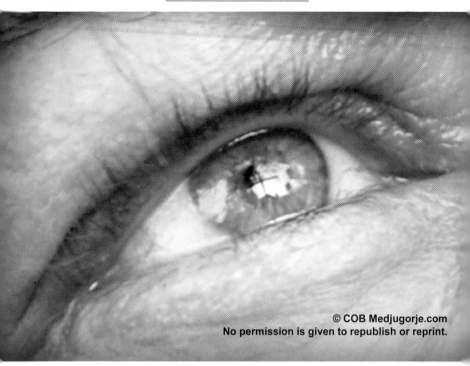

A close up was shown of Mirjana's eye, and a Friend of
Medjugorje wrote a short meditation about what Mirjana
sees when she sees Our Lady. Then people started to write to
us, saying that they were seeing "something" in the picture.

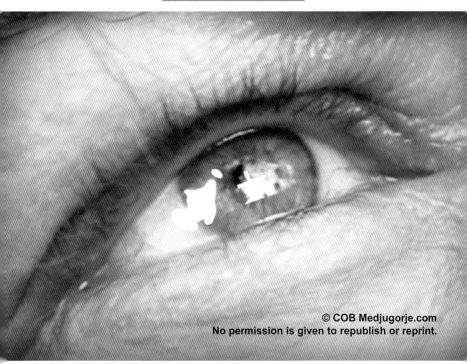

(Picture highlighted in white to see the image more clearly) —A Friend of Medjugorje is not prone to showing images like this, but, it was undeniable when the comments started to come in that there was more in the picture. On some websites, people were saying that it was merely a reflection. In response to these websites, other people were taking pictures of their own eyes, to prove that it would not show the same, as just a reflection. Needless to say, this became one of the most iconic images of the Second of the Month series. For more about this picture and many other things, be sure to watch the 6-minute presentation, *Why is Medjugorje Real?* on mej.com. *https://www.medjugorje.com/medjugorje-today/ medjugorje-headlines/why-is-medjugorje-real.html*

"On May 2, 1999, at 5 a.m. EST, there were seven of us before the Tabernacle in our church praying for all unbelievers as Our Lady asked…I had a sense of the Lord saying, "You have been faithful to this time of prayer since the beginning of the year…(1997)… Continue on...All we could do was weep and rest in His grace poured out through Our Lady…"

Great Falls, Virginia

May, 1999

108

Epilogue

from a Friend of Medjugorje

I began to speak and write about nonbelievers many years ago, when Our Lady first began giving messages concerning nonbelievers. I wrote that, we, all those who call ourselves followers of Our Lady, are also included in the ones Our Lady was referring to as nonbelievers. Some in the Medjugorje world rejected the notion that we all, even those reading Our Lady's messages every month, have nonbelief in us to some degree. Living in a world of modernism affects mentalities, with aspects of non-belief, even though many would deny it to be so. Some in the Medjugorje world even went so far as to write that the 25th messages were for Medjugorje believers, and the 2nd of the month messages were for nonbelievers, as if we were two separate groups. I immediately accepted that the

Second of the Month messages were first for me.
What nonbeliever was reading the Second of the
Month messages anyway? If they were not believers, they wouldn't be following Our Lady in the first
place. Who, then, was Our Lady giving the Second
of the Month messages for? I clearly understood
through years of cognition and experiences with
Our Lady, She was giving them for everyone. Our
Lady eventually confirmed what you just read. She
said on June 2, 2011:

> **"...As I call you to prayer for those
> who have not come to know the love
> of God, if you were to look into your
> hearts you would comprehend that I
> am speaking about many of you..."**

I could see plainly that Our Lady was here to
destroy every vestige of nonbelief in all hearts, everyone, with faith or no faith. Though Our Lady de-
fined to Mirjana that a nonbeliever is someone who
does not know the love of God, Our Lady is also

speaking to those of us who have known God's love because we have all been infected by the world's nonbelief to varying degrees. Our Lady is speaking to me, you and nonbelievers alike.

As I wrote in the book, <u>Big Q, Little Q: The Calm Before the Storm</u>, February 2019, Our Lady's plan is to bring us from the darkness to the Light. The Scriptures states:

> ***"Therefore, whatever you have said in the darkness will be heard in the light."*** Luke 12:3

There are many evil things in the world. Our Lady confirms this by Her words:

August 25, 1992

> **"...I call upon you to open yourselves completely to me, so that through each of you I may be enabled to convert and**

**save the world, where there is much sin
and many things that are evil…"**

There are evils in this world today that are
too heinous to even mention. But they cannot
remain in the darkness while Our Lady is here with
us to shed light. When some of these things become known, and they will become known, it will
be understood why Our Lady has come for all these
years and said, **"dear children," "little children,"
"my dear children," "my dear little children."**
Those who have discernment will understand. We
have a history with Our Lady, since 1981, that wher-
ever She goes, the Light goes.

Medjugorje visionary, Ivan, lives in Boston,
Massachusetts, in the USA. Our Lady appears
to Ivan every day when he is at home. When the
scandal in the Church surfaced in 2002, where was
the place the scandal broke open first in the United
States and for the whole world? Boston. Light and
dark cannot coexist. Our Lady, through Her appa-

ritions, forced the darkness out into the light. Our
Lady said on March 14, 1985:

> **"…in your life you have all experi-
> enced light and darkness. God grants
> to every person to recognize good
> and evil. I am calling you to the light,
> which you should carry to all the peo-
> ple who are in darkness. People who
> are in darkness daily come into your
> homes. Dear children, give them the
> light!"**

Our Lady has given a "witness" of what to do.
She brings the light and shows us that we should
do the same. Our Lady has promised the world a
century of peace:

December 25, 1999

> **"…Through your 'yes' for peace and
> your decision for God, a new possibil-
> ity for peace is opened. Only in this**

**way, little children, this century will
be for you a time of peace and well-
being…"**

Can a new peace come to the world with a
Communist China or North Korea, or a "treason-
ous deep state" and many other things in the world
which need to be addressed? What about "mega"
pharmaceutical companies and deceptive vaccines,
or the godless education system, or industrial farm-
ing, or the fake news, and a host of other things
that we have simply accepted to live with, even
if we don't like it or believe in it? What was the
coronavirus pandemic about? Making people stop
and reflect. Reflect about what? About what we
have been living with and tolerating in our lives.
These evils will be addressed by Our Lady in the
time that She is still with us. Those who pray for
discernment will understand those times when the
darkness is brought to light. There will be many
more things coming in the very near future that will

manifest this battle between light and dark. Do not be swayed by lying voices, nor intimidated by evil.

When I encouraged people to pray at the same time as Mirjana in Medjugorje, you have just read how the hatred of hell came against it. Why? Because people were getting up in the middle of the night and bringing light, "in the darkness of night." Those who have read these pages have seen, that all that was brought against Our Lady's mission at Caritas, particularly against me individually, did not stop us from moving ahead in the plan Our Lady was showing me to walk. Our Lady said:

November 25, 1987

> **"...If you do not pray, you shall not be able to recognize my love and the plans which God has for this parish and for each individual. Pray that satan does not entice you with his pride and deceptive strength..."**

We will not be enticed nor intimidated by satan and those who, through their actions, support his work, instead of Our Lady's plan. Follow Our Lady. She is leading us to the light.

January 2, 2007

"…Follow me and my luminous example…"

Many people have misinterpreted these words. What is Our Lady's "example?" Is Her example just what we read in the Scripture, that She was quiet and only prayed? Or is Our Lady's "luminous" example quite different? Our Lady is here to work. Her clothes are that of a servant. The color is grey, not the fancy adornments of a Queen.* She is here for a spring cleaning, turning everything upside down to be able to clean up every speck of dirt. Every time you see an event happening in the world today, such as what was exposed in Boston,

---

* In Medjugorje, the visionaries see Our Lady dressed in a simple grey gown and white veil, with no adornments.

where darkness is brought to the light, that is Our Lady's doing. Our Lady said:

January 25, 1997

"…This time is my time…"

Our Lady has this time, when the "clock has been turned back," to make more time, for a world in darkness, to bring it to the light. To follow Her example, is to do the same. Everyone is necessary and is called to this work to bring light, to bring conversion, to bring Our Lady, in the freedom to discern what and how they are to fulfill their part in Her plan.

November 2, 2016

"…The united love of my apostles will live, will conquer and will expose evil…" November 2, 2016

There will always be a battle between light and dark, but if we refuse to confront the darkness out of fear, indifference, convenience or to protect a position of influence, we will never do as Our Lady has commanded us: to break the darkness so that the Light of Her Son may shine through. We are called by Our Lady to be courageous.

> *"Greater is he that is in you, than he that is in the world."* 1 John 4:4

In the Seriousness of "This Time"
Taking HER Messages Seriously,

Friend of Medjugorje

Friend of Medjugorje

Postscript:

There have been a lot of people through the years who have suppressed Our Lady's messages and not taken them seriously. For them, Our Lady has given them their sentence; a sentence that has already been pronounced, that cannot be understood by them now, but will be understood in the future. Our Lady announced the sentence in Her August 25, 1997, message when She said:

> **"…now you do not comprehend this grace, but soon a time will come when you will lament for these messages…"**

The mission of Caritas is not the only thing that has been built and structured on Our Lady's messages, but a whole new way of life, bonded to the messages, that is lived by the Community of Caritas, all of which manifested from Our Lady's words. When I wrote the rule of the Community of Caritas for our bishop in 2001, who requested it,

I gave it the title, *"A Way of Life in A New Time"* because it is not so much a rule as it is "a way" of living the messages of Our Lady that is successful and unique in all of the Medjugorje world.

What has been stated in this book is sufficient to awaken people to the reality that there is a grave threat coming in the future. When the time comes for the release of the secrets, satan and all his minions in hell and on earth will attempt to delay the announcement of their release. Whether that delay is to the last moment before their release, or more so, until *after* the Secrets take place—the aim of the delay would be to steal the thunder of the secrets away from Our Lady by not allowing the secrets to be *foretold.*

If this happened, at the very least, it would minimize the time for the warning of the Secrets to be spread to the world's population. Because the devil cannot stop the Secrets from happening, his first choice would be to have the announcement come *after the Secrets occur*. The devil's second choice would be to delay their announcement as much as possible to eat up the time during the three days notice in order to minimize the spreading of the warning to the least number of people as possible. Again, to be explicitly clear of what will happen: satan will do anything and everything to delay the announcing of the release of the secrets. How can I be so certain? Chinese warrior, Sun Tzu, two thousand years ago, said, know your enemy. Who is the enemy? satan. The enemy of Our Lady. The enemy of Our Lady's plans.

These points are important to repeat. Why? The whole Medjugorje world must fast on bread and water for 7 days with Mirjana and Fr. Petar, the priest that Mirjana has chosen, in order to block satan's interference. So I repeat this very critical point: Since satan cannot stop the secrets from happening, and we know he can't, as Mirjana has stated the secrets <u>will happen</u>, he will work to diminish the effects of the secrets. Remember, Our Lady said that his power will be destroyed through the secrets—but that doesn't mean that he will not be able to wield his influence in such a way as to cheat Our Lady out of the greatest harvest possible by diminishing the numbers of conversions through devious means.

As already covered in the previous chapter, the question is: who could stop the secrets? Mirjana has said that the priest she chose to reveal the secrets to the world does not have a choice whether or not he will announce the secrets. He must reveal the secrets because it is God's will. Who, then, could stop Fr. Petar from revealing the secrets? Donald Trump, the President of the United States couldn't stop him. Nor could the President of Bosnia, or the mayor of Medjugorje. The only ones who could stop Fr. Petar are those who have legitimate authority over him. The history that has been revealed in these pages is for the sole purpose as to send a message. What is the message? Let not anyone even dare to think to delay or stop the secrets from being released.

Order Form

	The Plan for Nonbelievers from Dark to Light and the Resistance to It Soft Cover Books BF127	*(Please add shipping and handling)* ☐ 1=$4.00 ☐ 10=$30 ($3.00 EA) ☐ 25=$50 ($2.00 EA) ☐ 50=$75 ($1.50 EA) **NEW**	$
	"Medjugorje, Mirjana a Mystery is Revealed" Short Books BK1010	*Suggested Donation (Please add shipping and handling)* ☐ 1=FREE please add S&H ☐ 50=$17.50 (35¢ EA) ☐ 10=$5.00 (50¢ EA) ☐ 100=$30.00 (30¢ EA) ☐ 25=$10.00 (40¢ EA) ☐ 1,000=$300.00 (30¢ EA)	$
	The Corona Vision Soft Cover Books BF126	*(Please add shipping and handling)* ☐ 1=$4.00 ☐ 10=$30 ($3.00 EA) ☐ 25=$50 ($2.00 EA) ☐ 50=$75 ($1.50 EA) **NEW**	$
	"Prayer for Nonbelievers" PR1045 5"×7" Prayer Cards	*Suggested Donation (Please add shipping and handling)* ☐ 1=75¢ ☐ 100=$15.00 (15¢ EA) ☐ 10=$2.50 (25¢ EA) ☐ 500=$50.00 (10¢ EA) ☐ 50=$10.00 (20¢ EA) ☐ 1,000=$80.00 (8¢ EA)	$

Subtotal | $

Shipping & Handling

Order Sub-total	U.S. Mail (Standard)	UPS (Faster)
$0-$10.00	$5.00	$15.00
$10.01-$20.00	$7.50	$17.50
$20.01-$50.00	$10.00	$20.00
$50.01-$100.00	$15.00	$25.00
Over $100.00	15% of total	25% of total

For overnight delivery, call for pricing.
***International (Surface):**
Double above shipping Cost.
Call for faster International delivery.

$

CASES OF 100 BOOKS For Easy Convenience

The Plan for Nonbelievers from Dark to Light and the Resistance to it BF126–CASE CASES OF 100 ($1.00 EA) $100 + $45 S&H = $145.00	*(UPS Shipping is included)* Cases QTY. TOTAL ☐ 1 100 $145.00 ☐ 2 200 $290.00 ☐ OTHER _____ ($145.00 EA)	$
The Corona Vision BF126–CASE CASES OF 100 ($1.00 EA) $100 + $45 S&H = $145.00	*(UPS Shipping is included)* Cases QTY. TOTAL ☐ 1 100 $145.00 ☐ 2 200 $290.00 ☐ OTHER _____ ($145.00 EA)	$

TOTAL: | $

☎ Ph: (Outside USA add 001)
205-672-2000 ext. 315 USA 24 hrs.
🖷 Fax: **205-672-9667 USA 24 hrs.**

📬 Mail: **Caritas of Birmingham**
100 Our Lady Queen of Peace Drive
Sterrett, AL 35147-9987 USA

Enclose in remittance envelope or call in your order and donation.
If you have any questions you may call 205-672-2000 and leave a message on ext. 315.
Or call during office hours 8:30 a.m.–5:00 p.m. Central Time
Monday–Friday and talk with a real person ☺

The Federal Tax Exempt I.D. # for Caritas of Birmingham is 63-0945243.

Ship to: Name(s) (please print) _____ Birthday: _____

Address _____

City _____ State _____ Zip Code _____

Phone # _____(if an international number, include all digits)

☐ Payment Enclosed

Credit Card type (check one) ☐ VISA ☐ MasterCard ☐ Discover

Credit Card Number ☐☐☐☐ ☐☐☐☐ ☐☐☐☐ ☐☐☐☐   3-Digit Code on Back: ☐☐☐

Expiration date: ☐☐-☐☐   e-mail: _____